Laura G. Collins

Immortelles and Asphodels

Laura G. Collins

Immortelles and Asphodels

ISBN/EAN: 9783337370503

Printed in Europe, USA, Canada, Australia, Japan

Cover: Foto ©Andreas Hilbeck / pixelio.de

More available books at **www.hansebooks.com**

Immortelles and Asphodels

POEMS

BY

LAURA G. COLLINS

CINCINNATI
THE ROBERT CLARKE COMPANY
1898

TO

MY TWO LITTLE GRANDNIECES,

SISTERS,

LAURA CASE COLLINS

AND

MARGARET ECKSTEIN GREGG,

AGED RESPECTIVELY

EIGHT AND SIX YEARS.

INDEX.

This Day,	7
A Phantom Realm,	10
Freeholder, The Little and I,	14
The Pines,	16
What Makes the May?	19
My Lawn,	22
Peaches and Cream,	28
The Autumn Drive,	32
October,	36
The Brothers,	39
Little Phil,	43
Little Betty,	47
One of Life's Strange Episodes,	50
Preces,	54
The Only One,	56
Here and There,	58
How Do They Forget?	60
In Memoriam,	62
We Know,	64
My Friend,	66
Musings,	70

Blind—Oh !—Blind,	70
Thoughts on Life,	71
The Indians,	79
Kansas,	82
Adrift,	87
An Episode of Travel,	90
A Madrigal,	91
Paolina,	92
Ludwig, der King. Louis, the King. The Mad King of Bavaria,	94
Egypt,	97
The Alps,	102
Immortelles and Asphodels,	106

POEMS.

This Day.

Into the hazy distance melt
  The old Ohio Hills;
The river at their feet glides on
  And all the valley fills,
    While bendeth tenderly and true
    O'erhead the sky so blue.

The ancient town in sunlight steeped
  Seems wrapped in dreamless sleep.
No creature, tread, or any sound,
  Doth break the silence deep,
    While bendeth tenderly and true
    O'erhead the sky so blue.

A Sabbath stillness rests on earth;
   Hills, river, town, the air,
Are cased in crystal as it were,
   Or some enchantment rare,
      While bendeth tenderly and true
      O'erhead the sky so blue.

Into the distance follows slow
   The gazer's lingering glance,
Then loitering, musing, takes in all
   As one lost in a trance,
      While bendeth tenderly and true
      O'erhead the sky so blue.

The heaven above, the earth beneath,
   The air, the perfect day,
The gazer's exaltation—all—
   How soon they pass away,
      While bendeth tenderly and true
      O'erhead the sky so blue.

What means this fair, familiar scene,
   This sleep, or trance, or dream?

THIS DAY.

Holds it a veiled significance?
  Is it some mood supreme?
    While bendeth tenderly and true
    O'erhead the sky so blue.

Not depths of revery reveal,
  Not keenest search doth gain
Solution for this mystery
  That haunts and goads the brain,
    While bendeth tenderly and true
    O'erhead the sky so blue.

A Phantom Realm.

No potentate, empress, am I, or queen,
No crown on my brow is ever seen;
But I have a realm that is all my own
I would not exchange for a crown and a throne.

In the heart of a mighty forest it stands,
And ever the blue sky and sunshine commands.
The trees in that crystal empyrean rise
To heights that mock the most far-reaching eyes.

The vast space hedged in by the rampart they make
Doth Beauty's bewildering devices take
Of flower-beds, arbors, grottos and groves
Wherever the gazer's enchanted glance roves.

The first are in squares with borders of green,
Peering forth from which Youth's charming faces are seen,
While rising above them, great masses within,
Unknown, nameless, flowers a startled gaze win—

Pure white with a rim of Cupids so tiny, so fair,
The wonder awakes how they can be there.
In another, stalks studded the length of the stem
With blooms that outmarvel the rarest of gems.

With reflected petals in colors so gay,
And stamens and pistils that end in a way
No botany shows—the daintiest fringe,
Each thread of which holds as though hung on a hinge.

A fairy-like, magical, wee silver bell
Which touched by the faintest breath at once doth swell
To a musical tinkle that holds spellbound the ear
Of every listener it allures to draw near.

A mother-of-pearl grotto, mistletoe overgrown
With pearl—bestrung sprays, is the next wonder shown.
An arbor of honey-suckles, its perfume of spice,
Clouds of humming-birds flashing like jewels entice.

There, near by, a grove, its trees solid gold,
Agleam with gold lilies a gold mist doth enfold.
Afar through that forest wall an opening is made,
A vanishing distance of leafy arcade—

Beyond which an Arctic scene rises to view.
Ice caverns with the green of the emerald's hue,
Archways of the lapis lazuli's blue light,
Blazing grottos of diamonds blinding the sight,

'Gainst a background of mountains covered with snow,
From the crests of which waterfalls leap far below—

'Tis gone! This realm of mine, weird, unique,
How vain should any essay it to seek,
For it is a Phantom Realm, yet all my own,
That I would not exchange for a crown and a throne.

The Little Freeholder and I.

On the very tip of the topmost spray
   Of my stately pine tree sat a bird,
And as I listened to him one day
   This colloquy strange I dreamed or heard.

The while he was piping he sat and swung
   With a pretty grace as the breeze stole by,
And the slender spray to which he clung
   Re-echoed his strain with its gentle sigh.

He was unconscious or else did not care,
   As he gazed around from his airy height,
That I of his presence was quite aware,
   For he piped away with a merry might.

I smiled and quite softly said: " Little bird
   " Do you know who owns that swing on the pine ?"

His song seemed to answer me word for word:
"Yes, I know—I know—it is thine and mine."

"How now, pretty one, you must be in fun,
Or lively perhaps on the dew of the vine!
A copartnership I am sure there is none;
So pray tell me how you have share in the pine."

The sauce-box! He ruffled nor feather nor note,
As I waited to hear what reply he could make,
So softly—so swiftly—it swelled from his throat,
"What the Father provides us I surely may take."

The Pines.
(A Home near Philadelphia.)

Who planted you, O, solemn pines
   A hundred years ago?
Who o'er you watched with anxious care
   When you began to grow?

When first your polished spears of green
   Escaped the guardian sod,
Whose feet long perished from the earth,
   Then all around you trod.

With journeys oft which bending form,
   Which eager searching eye—
Mother's, or sire's, or little one's,
   Was the first to espy?

What subtle motive moved within
   The heart of him who chose
You o'er all trees and placed you here
   In dark, funereal rows?

THE PINES.

Was it ambition that you should
   Become ancestral trees,
Waving o'er the ancestral home
   Through distant centuries?

Or singleness of forethought that
   Though not his blood or name,
Still some one's children's children should
   Enjoy you all the same?

Methinks 'twere this; but now my heart
   Went forth in grateful thought
To him unknown who in the past
   This deed of kindness wrought.

You stand in stately solemn might,
   Majestic o'er all trees,
And in your boughs the minstrel winds
   Wake ceaseless harmonies.

Your overshadowing branches make
   A dim, cathedral shade,
And God's own temple you do seem
   By human hands not made.

A sacred stillness broods within
    The space you thus enclose,
And nought less holy e'er intrudes
    To break this deep repose.

(This avenue of pines was said to be the oldest—over a hundred years old—and the finest in eastern Pennsylvania.)

What Makes the May?

What makes the May,—the lovely May,
    The pet month of the year—
    The one to earth most dear.
The tender, windsome, gladsome May,
The famed, fair, flowery May?
          What makes the May?

The Bards of Eld—made they the May?
    They crowned her in their rhymes.
    Innumerable times—
An odorous, floral Queen—sweet May!
The Bards?—nay—they made not the May!
          Made not the May!

The Birds before the Bards their lay
    Trilled sweetly forth alway,
    But sweetest in the May,
The old poetic legends say.
Yet they—the Birds made not the May;
          Made not the May!

WHAT MAKES THE MAY?

The flowers that bloom only in May
    As though earth bore but flowers
    To grace her glowing hours,
Aye, myriad flowers to crowd the May—
Yet they—the flowers—make not the May.
        Made not the May.

The Breezes blow softest in May—
    Their dainty harps are hung
    Her silvery sprays among;
And with her waste of blossoms they
Make merry play—but do not make the May,
        Make not the May!

Sunniest suns shine down in May,
    And golden glories weave
    Where boughs their beams receive
On hillsides green in valleys gay,
But suns and sunshine make not May,
        Make not the May.

Oh! the blue skies that shield the May!
    That bend so clear above,
    Our heaven of hope and love,

Of all the bluest come in May.
Yet skies—blue skies—make not the May,
>> Make not the May.

The young May moon that shines in May
> And only in the May—
> That fails not of her sway
However roll the years away;
Moons—young May moons—make not the May.
>> What makes the May!

The fresh blithe hearts that ope in May,
> That throb with trust and ruth,
> That brim with hope and truth,
Glad smiles and shining eyes—ah! they
The May makes them and they make May—
>> These make the May!

My Lawn.

I 'VE a green spreading lawn which the fairies
    Come at night, I am sure, to trip o'er,
For each morn I detect dainty traces
    I never have seen there before;
A spangle danced off in the darkness,
    Flashes still in the cedar's dense shade,
And some magic, weird, cunning clings to it;
    It ever my clasp doth evade;—

A slipper left there by some loiterer
    Late roused to wild haste by the dawn;
No pinafore darling's doll-baby
    Could ever that wee thing get on,—
A tress of gold floss on the brier,
    A shred of the silveriest gauze
Some fairy maid's scarf torn in passing,
    Or love-gage dropped there in the pause.

When she leant to her lover's low wooing
  In some nook sheltered quite from the crowd.
I can see him, the sly roguish fellow!
  As he stands there exultant and proud.
A ripple of smiles lights his features,
  But tenderness beams from his eyes,
And he gently bends over—low—lower—
  And echoes her shy, happy sighs.

The wee things!—they twinkle and vanish,
  But this strand wove of silver and mist
Is a proof the most cynical doubter
  Of fairy folk can not resist.
Ah! there is more to one patient in watching;—
  Who will wait for their own witching hour
On a night when the moonlight is brightest
  Many glimpses may catch of their power.

There 's a fitting of figures as brilliant
  As fireflies flashing at eve,
A twinkling of music from instruments
  No mortal thought ere did conceive.

Some dance to their measures, while others
    Flit in light or in shadow at will,
And some in the hedges' dark corners
    Hold us spellbound with trials of skill.

One heaps sand in his hand's tiny hollow—
    Grain by grain he hurls forth little stars,
Shining sparklets that swiftly in systems
    Revolve where no doubting ere mars.
Another quick catches a dew-drop
    Trembling hung to some flower's closed bloom—
In a breath with swift puffs and strange passes
    Wreathed masses of clouds upward loom.

With a quaint, comic magic another
    Hovers 'round till some web just begun
By a trim, traveled spider is finished
    And most rarely with dew-drops bestrung—
When—presto!—you' re watching, but see not,
    The conjury quicker than sight—
It is swept from the bush in a twinkling,
    And floats—a balloon—in the light.

While the saucy young aeronaut in it
    Its gossamer cables soon cuts,
Cooly stretches himself at the bottom,
    And one eye at a time archly shuts.
While the other flames out on the spider
    Delight and defiance at once,
'Till, baffled, bewildered, it rolls up
    Its trim, traveled self, like a dunce.

Ah! my wide-spreading lawn, in the daytime,
    You lie smooth and green to the view,
And only the fairies and I know
    What happens of nights upon you.
What revels fill up your fair spaces,
    What new plans of frolic unfold,
What adventures in far distant places
    With gay shouts of laughter are told.

How welcome to all your rare lovliness!
    To the slope leading down to the lake,
To the terraced bank where the verbenas
    Of bright hues a gay mat-work make;

To the levels beneath my tall tulips
   Where they dance to bewildering sounds;
To the dimples beyond the catalpas,
   The plateaus on the top of the mounds;—

To the broad, graveled avenue winding
   'Neath the aspen tree's quivering shade,
Where to their watch my old lions couchant
   Full a century ago down laid;
To the thickets of cedar and hemlock
   Rimmed with clumps of gold lilies so tall,
Though scores of such wee folk a ladder were made,
   They would mock still the topmost of all

Ah! they are welcome—wee, wonderful fairies—
   For children I have none to enjoy;
All the magic which nature and art here
   The summer long seem to employ.
Yet—I group them so oft by the lilies,
   On the roots gnarled and old of the trees,
And I am startled at times by the ringing
   Of children's glad shouts on the breeze.

MY LAWN.

Oft I hear airy names called and answers
   As lightly flung out in return,
As I strain my gaze far toward the forest
   Where they play "hide-and-seek" in the fern.
Sometimes, too, I see them grow weary,
   Then they laughing and panting seek me,
To drop down on the grass where I'm sitting
   And lay their tired little heads on my knee.

Ah! the vision of them that comes oftenest
   Is of little forms fading away—
Of shining fest that gleam far and vanish—
   In the light of a more perfect day?
We may think it—must think it—God help us!—
   My fairies, I shall need you to-night.
O! wide-spreading lawn, far too lonesome—
   O! heart, shadowed thus from the light.

Peaches and Cream.

Was she a beauty?—for you did not say—
The maiden across the table that day,
With her pet colt gathered under her arm,
Safely sheltered from every harm,
    And feeding it with a steady stream
    Of hugs and kisses and—peaches and
cream!

It—her pet, her joy, and her pride—
Cutting the sunshine and grass outside,
Entered that banqueting-hall with the air
Of the guest most honored and welcomed there,
    Sure 't would be fed with that steady stream
    Of hugs and kisses and—peaches and
cream!

And—was it my idle brush to redeem—
For this is the way it to me did seem—

You requested that I would paint that scene
Through your eyes which lent such a glamor and sheen
  To the maiden who fed with that steady stream
   Of hugs and kisses and—peaches and cream!

They fairly flashed as you told of the pair,
So I infer she was young and know she was fair;
And it—why it may have grown up to be
Peer, rival, yea more—ahead of Jay Eye-See!
  Despite or because of that steady stream
   Of hugs and kisses and—peaches and cream.

Yes, it is as plain as plain can be
The thing might be done quite cleverly;
And my fingers are tingling at your behest
To do it, and do indeed their "level best"
  On the maiden feeding that steady stream
   Of hugs and kisses and—peaches and cream!

And the cunning dare-devil bit of a colt—
Not half believe me, so much of a dolt
As that other guest who sat there and stared
Instead of trying to—get himself paired
    That he too might feed a steady stream
        Of hugs and kisses and—peaches and cream!

The banquet, host, hostess, other guests and he
Out-doors all sunshine, in-doors all glee!
'T is a picture that paints itself by the mind's eye,
And why not by the brush in the near by and by,
    With the maiden intent on that steady stream
        Of hugs and kisses and—peaches and cream!

But sitting and thinking I thought I'd first do
A pen-sketch by way (maybe) of showing you

My pen is as potent as my brush any time
If I do n't have to bother about rhythm and rhyme,
> Which do n't always run in as steady a stream
> As hugs and kisses and—peaches and cream!

[Written for a bachelor friend (who witnessed the incident), January 12, 1885, after 11 at night.]

The Autumn Drive.

("Two Giddy Young Things on Pleasure Bent.")

Over the hills and through the hollows,
   Behind our spirited steeds we went;
Not asking, nor caring, who leads? who follows?
"Two giddy young things on pleasure bent."

"Two giddy young things" (!) alas! for the roses,
   The brilliant bloom of their Long Ago.
Alas! that a wrinkle now reposes
   Where only a dimple was wont to show.

Alas! that tresses of blond and brown,
   Which over each youthful brow once made
A glory greater than a queen's crown
   Are now with streaks of silver inlaid.

N'importe! we'll take the goods provided
  By God beneficent if unknown;
And stand to our colors though derided
  Because our youth's fresh charms are flown.

This day—a day of God's own making—
  The broad green earth, soft air, blue sky—
As we gaze there comes an awaking,
  A stir of the soul both deep and high.

This beautiful earth—we love it so!
  And most our own little corner here;
Yonder mountain peaks that dreamlike show
  Even in sunshine so bright and clear.

This pretty tangle of hills all round,
  Some shorn and shaven, some covered still
With groves where shy Dryads might be found •
  Could we turn them out in a modern mill.

Thicket and dingle, dale and ravine—
  A ravishment to both smell and sight—
Wide stretching fields in brown, gold and green,
  Odors of wild things and wild flowers bright.

Daises late blooming, Sweet Williams too,
  And Black-eyed Susans gayest of all,
Clad in gold raiment, spic-span, brand new;
  And purple iron weed slender and tall.

More might be mentioned, but I refrain,
  Because of countless charms that await
Every glance as we speed to enchain,
  Every thought fresh pleasure to freight.

Farm houses set amid clumps of shade trees;
  Beautified hill-slope, knoll and low vale;
In pools crinkled here and there by the breeze
  Flocks of white ducks with golden legs sail.

Coasting the creeks far vistas delight
  In depths of greenery dusky and dim;
Islets appear in the slanting sunlight
  Rounded in outlines dainty and trim.

Fresh pictures flash and each one reveals
  Regions of beauty undreamed of and fair,
A rapture ecstatic over us steals—
  Ah! had Eden itself visions more rare?

We measured the miles with talk and musing,
  We read our delight in each other's eyes,
And marked each scene for fear of losing
  Secrets of nature that we would prize.

Low sank the sun, soft fell the twilight,
  Over the world stole a tender flush;
And as slowly crept onward the night
  Upon our spirits fell a deep hush.

Day of all days, we set you apart,
  One that we would not, could not, forget
One consecrated in each other's heart,
  Forever—ay, till Life's sun shall set.

October, 1897.

How the leaves are coming down!
In the country, in the town,
Golden, purple, crimson, brown—
How the leaves are coming down!
From the elms a tawny green,
From the poplars gold is seen,
While the maples' brilliant sheen
Flashes dazzling flames between.

How the breezes come and go!
Some with swift and merry flow,
Some murmuring, sad and slow,
How the breezes come and go!
From the North a frosty chill,
From the East an answering thrill,
But the South sweet violets fill,
And the West's a zephyr still.

OCTOBER—1897.

How the birds in flocks appear
As their southward flight draws near
In this fall-time of the year,
In the yellow leaf and sere.
As far as doth roam the eye
In black lines against the sky,
Following their leader's cry,
Zigzag, high and low, they fly.

Sounds of insects in the air,
Sounds that make a music rare,
Little creatures debonnaire,
Humming, hopping, leaping there.
How they sing and buzz and hide
In the brown fields far and wide—
In the sunny, warm noon-tide—
How they hum and buzz and hide!

How the sunshine slips away
In a dream the livelong day,
While its mist of gold doth lay
Like a veil till twilight gray.

OCTOBER—1897.

Softly, tranquilly, doth fall
A hush—a silence—upon all.
Effort, will, under a pall,
Speech and thought are held in thrall.

How earth owns October's reign!
Watching day by day its train
Of fruits, flowers and golden grain.
How it builds—castles in Spain!
Dazed with the enchanted air
It forgets all carking care,
Feeling sure that every-where
Life is just as sweet and fair.

And such idle dreamers!—We
Gaze and muse in ecstasy
On the wondrous scene we see,
Vaguely asking can it be
A part of the world we know,
Or perchance, some wizard show
With its glamour veiled in glow
As we dreamers come and go!

The Brothers.

Not so many winters' snows,
    Not so many summers' suns,
The history of their young lives shows
    As through memory it runs.

Twice a twelwe-month came between
    One birthday that served the twain,
When October's golden sheen
    Charms the senses e'en to pain.

"All nerves and quicksilver, Frank,"
    Said the father by and by.
"And Hercules our Will might thank
    Any goddess to supply."

So they grew, the elder still
    Slight and nervous, bright and quick,
And the younger, sturdy Will,
    Right-hand man in prank and trick.

And they loved each other so—
    Never thought came but of two;
What one asked for well he knew
    Would the other plead for too.

Where the long grass longest grew
    On the pleasant, sunny lawn,
Two small mowers met the view,
    Morn by morn, at early dawn.

Two small sickles flashed about,
    Seemingly with steady sweep—
Ah! The laughter that rang out
    Still my memory doth keep.

What though sheaves and stacks were small,
    Two young hearts delighted were,
Shouting, "Mamma, see how tall!"
    Sure of smiles and praise from *her*.

What boy never climbed a tree?
    How they would have pitied such.
"Birds' nests," was their frequent plea,
    "Mamma, just to see, not touch."

Or, "Yon great red apple there
  On that big limb, most in reach,
Mamma, sure you will not care,"
  Always both would thus beseech.

Where the boat in waiting lay
  On the lake by willows rimmed,
Two small boatmen day by day
  Bravely o'er its waters skimmed.

Side by side did gayly row,
  Throwing in some tricks for fun,
Such as rocking to and fro,
  Low next to the timid one.

Sometimes shooting on the shore
  Hard enough to tip out both;
Then splashing each other o'er,
  For a ducking nothing loth.

One supreme day "Pony" came,
  And for all his looks demure,
Shy, bright eye, and gentle name,
  Up to any prank, be sure.

"Papa, did you think—come see—
    Things would come to such a pass?"
Papa laughed, then rolled all three
    In mad frolic on the grass.

"Pony tossed us overhead,
    Could we help it, mamma, pray?"
Eagerly both of them said,
"So we we thought we'd have a play."

What wild scampers down the lane,
    Where the weeping elm-trees swayed,
Wild tossed curls and streaming mane
    Flashing through the cool, dense shade.

Summer days why flit so fast,
    Shine of golden suns why fade?
Hours of joy why thus soon past?
    Hath naught ne'er your flight delayed?

Little Phil.

WHAT has become of "Little Phil"
   Since the years when he stood at my knee,
In his earnest endeavor to learn
   His first lesson in A, B, C?

Never an idler, Little Phil,
   I see you again and again
Poring absorbed over slate or book
   While clutching your pencil or pen.

Never behindhand, Little Phil,
   When the questions were passed around,
In a concentrated, careful way
   You were first who the answers found.

Well I recall one "showing-off" hour,
   In your kindergarten term;
Alone you stood for your class under fire,
   Unconscious, gentle, and firm.

"Listen," said the teacher; "tell what you
    hear."
  You bowed your head lower and bent
    your ear.
  These were the grave words that our ears
    did greet:
    "I hear big wagons rumbling through the
      street."

"Try again," said the teacher; "tell us once
    more."
  Your child face a growing interest wore,
As you listened intently as before:
    "I hear morn and evening the great can-
      nons' roar."

"Well done," cried the teacher; "once again
    try."
  With your wrapt gaze riveted on high,
In measured, solemn tones came the reply:
    "I hear the thunder up in the sky."

"'His mind is burning with great ideas,"
    Said the teacher in admiring amaze;

"And if it works thus ere he is six years old,
　Given life, what will it do some of these days?"

The years are gone, but memory survives,
　And oftimes I live them again,
　Asking, "What has become of Little Phil?
　Is he somewhere a man among men?"

"Does manhood the childhood's promise fulfill
　Which was shown that morning in school?
　Is the man he has grown to from Little Phil
　As docile to Duty's rule?"

"Does he listen and hear with the inner ear,
　And catch now such sounds sublime?
　Accords the spirit of the mature man
　With the spirit of that early time?"

These questions have haunted me, Little Phil,

Since our pathways went far asunder
Now many and many a year ago—
Will they ever have answer, I wonder?

[The "big wagons" were the transportation wagons used in our Civil War.

The "great cannons" were those of the Barracks at Newport, Ky.]

Little Betty.

Great brown eyes with lightning flashes,
Softened by the long dark lashes;
   Lips as ripest cherries red;
Feet like fairies, hands with dimples,
Laugh like sound of stream that wimples
   In cascades o'er rocky bed.

Years and years their circles ended
Have with one another blended,
   In the distant dreamy Past,
Since death's marble fixed each feature
Of that gladsome, sunbright creature
   Whom my memory holds so fast.

Seven summers did she number
Ere she lay down in that slumber,
   Deeper than her baby sleep;

When the snow lay not more chilling
While my own young heart was thrilling
　With strange tears I could not weep.

Five and twenty years have vanished
Yet have not the image banished
　Of my little playmate dear.
For to-day I saw her smiling—
Heard that soft child voice beguiling
　Me with accent low and clear.

Under my closed eyelids stealing
Seemed that little child form kneeling
　With the old glance bent on me.
The wee hands with mine were playing,
And the red young lips were saying
　Some low spirit entreaty.

Strange! for *her* Heaven's open portal,
And the light and life immortal,
　Claimed and called and crowned so soon!
But for *me* gray hairs are gleaming.
On my brow and wrinkles seeming
　In the strife of earth's fierce noon.

Well for her the crown and glory !
And the earth old touching story,
  "Whom the gods love stay not here."
And for me not less well surely
End but Life's ordeal purely
  I may join her without fear.

One of Life's Strange Episodes.

His picture there upon the wall
   Sometimes I fix my gaze on it,
And all the fading past recall,
   As in a revery I sit.
Long years ago while yet a child,
   My father's friend he came and went,
Nor seemed to see me as he smiled
   And absently above me bent.

For sorrow's blight had early laid
   Its ruthless, crushing touch on him,
And still its shadow overweighed
   And all life's light and joy made dim
Through maidenhood he often came,
   And slowly with more cheerful mien,
Years bringing him success and fame
   His thoughts from the sad past did wean.

ONE OF LIFE'S STRANGE EPISODES. 51

Thus meeting, parting, time swept by
   Till from that home I went a bride.
He won another presently
   To share his place and pride.
Ah! brief my span of blissful years,—
   Death did not spare my Paradise.
The blow—the anguish beyond tears—
   The loss that yet for solace cries—

   .   .   .   .   .

A score of years passed by and more
   Before again our pathways crossed,
Far from the happy home of yore,
   We talked of what we'd won and lost.
Of all the freighted years had brought,—
   Rich gifts, the choicest and best,
Persistently desired and sought,
   Though sorrow's canker curb the zest.

A little rift in rush of talk;
   Silence as full as it could hold
Of thoughts that all expression mocks :—
   And then—so sudden swift he told

The old, old story—had he dared
   He would have tried to win me.
He blushed—a boy!—as thus he bared
   That youthful romance shyly.

A pause—and then another theme,
   Friends firmer, truer than before.
Knowing well his tender dream
   Was as futile as of yore.
The fair day sped; the sunshine waned;
   Creeping gloom veiled earth, lake, sky,
Where but now its glow had reigned
   Weaving spells of witchery.

Words sped—those lost we can not spare,
   Plans for meeting soon again,
Not on one projected there
   Shadow fell of coming pain.
One was that beyond the sea—
   Both were going—soon should meet
In climes renowned and comrades be;
   In turn seeking each famed seat.

Of science, art, and learning—all
    Man has guarded well and long;
And seek too each enchanted view
    Known through pencil, brush and song.
With warmth of word and grasp of hand
    And with unprophetic soul
We parted. Ah! no magic wand
    From our eyes fate's veil did roll.

  .   .   .   .   .

A fortnight—maybe less or more—
    Time a blank was when I read—.
"Over a book seeming to pore
    Our great senator found dead."

Preces.

MOONLIGHT folding earth
   In a clasp benign,
Aching human hearts
   Need thy peace divine!

Rain-drops falling down
   On the eager land,
Thirsty human soil
   Craves thy blessing bland!

Winds that rise and blow
   In the summer heat,
Let thy soft wings cool
   Pulses' fevered beat!

Shadows of all things—
   Cloud, or mount, or tree—
May thy mystic forms
   Blessings ever be!

Answering shape of cloud,
   Flying o'er the field,
Mark where weary heads
   Claim thy grateful shield!

Phantom of the mount
   Stretched on burning plain,
Travelers shelter seek
   In thy dim domain!

Thickest shade of woods
   Whereso'er you fall
Fainting human forms
   For thy largess call!

So of all things good,
   Beautiful and strong,
Let thy balm be poured
   On all need and wrong!

Heed these prayers that spring
   From our fainting souls;
Answer them in grace
   That inspires—consoles!

The Only One.

A LITTLE chair beside my own,
   A wee form sitting in it,
A sweet child-voice when we're alone
   Outsinging thrush or linnet.

A little hand trust into mine,
   A child's continuous chatter,
Blue eyes alight with love divine,
   And small feet's restless patter.

A little snow-white, curtained bed,
   A chest of childish playthings,
Some shelves of books "just made," she said,
   "For little ones and great kings."

A flitting, flashing fay or sprite
   That comes and goes at pleasure,
Making the very sunshine bright,
   My one—one—earthly treasure.

A dream—no more—she comes no more—
   And what is there remaining?
A life the tempest has swept o'er,
   And—thanks!—now swiftly waning.

Here and There.

Wave after wave forever flowing,
   River, dark river of doom,
One by one our darlings are going—
   Hidden so soon in thy gloom.

Beam after beam silently failing,
   O, Sun, that sets in the night—
Ray after ray we watch the veiling
   Of eyes that hold all our light.

Pang upon pang, sore-bruised and riven,
   O, Heart, is every tie:
Again, again, till all who were given,
   In Death's strange stillness lie.

Clod after clod fearfully heaping,
   O, Earth, thy cover is spread,
As side by side we lay them sleeping,
   Our idolized helpless dead.

Plash upon plash till Heaven's own strand,
    O, River of Life, is thine;
One by one till a radiant band,
    Our darlings, there doth shine.

Beam after beam, lighter and lighter,
    God's glory doth so increase;
Eyes from Death's shadow brighter and brighter,
    Aglow with Peace, Perfect Peace.

Thrill after thrill, ecstatic gladness,
    Heart, through each fiber doth leap.
What to thee now the vanished sadness?
    What that elsewhere thou didst weep?

Clod after clod, Death's mansion crumbleth,
    Grave, thy victory is o'er,
Earth's still sleepers, the highest, humblest,
    Rise to joy forever more.

How do they forget?

Why it is just as plain
Through this dreamy mist of summer rain
   That scene of a few brief months ago,
   In the midst of the bitter St. Agnes snow,
When the fair young bride of a honeymoon
Was claimed and taken away so soon,
   With that wild cry—I can hear it yet—
   Escaping her lips—"Do n't let him forget!"

Yet it is he that stands
In yon curtained alcove clasping hands
   With another, maybe, as fair and bright,
   Who sits by his side in the failing light.
He bends with the old, soft worshiping air—
Does he whisper the same sweet nothings there?—
   I can but see—yes, there lips have met—
   O! fair young bride, how can he forget?

HOW DO THEY FORGET?

As I think, another,
Tender and lovely, wife and mother,
    Stands out clear from the crypt of the years,
    For a moment only—tears, ah! tears—
He died, time passed—would we had lain her
By him ere there was aught to stain her!
    In shame her glory of womanhood set;—
    Woman, wife, mother—how could you forget?

Hark! from the parlor there
Bursts a bridal-peal of laughter rare.
    Gladsome and free from all care is its ring
    As the trill of birds in the budding spring.
Yet scarce, I think, has a twelve month flown
Since that same voice made wildest moan
    By a husband's grave—has it lost regret?
    Widowed, wedded—how does she forget?

In Memoriam.

[Written on the death of a lovely woman whom I never knew, Mrs. Bushrer Goshorn.]

THE fragrance of her lovely life
   All womanhood may claim
The right to speak with gentleness
   And reverence her name;
The sacred sense of sisterhood
   With one so pure and rare,
The touch as of a holy hand
That would its gladness share.

Her path illumed with light divine
   Shed by the soul within,
Arrested, wooed, and others won
   To seek and walk therein.
Why were you so relentless, Death?
   Why in such haste, O! Grave?
Not all of love could baffle you;
   Not all its efforts save.

Yet one thing—one—is left of her
    Not even you may chill—
The memory of her perfect life
    Is our possession still.
The dull combustion of our souls
    It stirs to glow and flame.
New goals, new aims, new plans unfold
    The best to do and claim.

We Know.

With wont and use
Scarce or profuse,
Through lapse or lack of ages,
The sword will rust
And sheathed in dust
Flame but on history's pages.

The finest point
Oil doth anoint,
The sharpest edge e'er fashioned
Will wear away,
So day by day
Do pangs the most impassioned.

With change and years
The bitterest tears
Are softened in their flowing;
The heart's long strain,
Grief's crushing reign,
Relax without our knowing.

WE KNOW.

    The deep wound heals,
    The smart time steals,
The darkest hour grows lighter,
      Hearts howe'er rent
      Learn such content
As makes their burden lighter.

    The clouds will rend,
    The blue heavens bend,
To bless the mournfulest gazing—
      Ah! shall not we
      Gaze truest
With hearts for only praising?

My friend.

I miss him from my life,
    The friend of many years—
A loss for which is no relief,
    Not even that of tears.

The mornings rare are flown
    When we, in commune high,
Talked on all themes that touch
    Our human destiny.

The strolls of later hours
    Upon his "green hill-top,"
Where challenges of bloom and scent,
    Our very breaths did stop.

The pauses brief or long
    That we scarce conscious made,
To mark the scene so fair
    Beneath his fruit trees' shade.

The mountains dim and blue
    That sometimes shone so clear,
Were those where he when life was young
    Hunted the antlered deer.

The hills that nearer ranged
    In links and chains unwound,
And shaped by glaciers in an age
    For which no date is found,

Had been familiar tramps of ours
    From childhood's early days,
And still for us a magic had
    That held the roving gaze.

The slower loiterings
    Amid his vines and flowers,
Where he with loving hand
    Would prune and work for hours.

Then from that outside world
    In-doors his books we sought,
To read and talk and sit,
    Losing ourselves in thought.

MY FRIEND.

His books—what friends they were!
   Homer—but Shakespeare first—
He oft recalled the day
   His wonders on him burst.

From all the centuries
   Their masters his own made;
Their words, worth, wisdom, wit,
   Forever with him stayed.

The evenings with the stars!
   From sweep of grassy lawn
We watched them rise and set,
   Through twilight on till dawn.

Such comradeship from Youth to Age,
   Such mingling of our best,
A consecration made of Life
   And all our meetings blessed.

I miss him from my life—
   The path is long behind,
But forward short and shorter grows
   And soon the end will find.

Beyond!—To what we go?—
    Still baffles human quest,
And mystery profound
    All effort doth invest.

Yet still we dream our dreams,
    And with the problem cope;
Yet still we build our Faiths
    Of Love, and Trust, and Hope.

I miss him from my life—
    . . . . . .
. . . .
    . . . . . .

Musings.

When I am gone they will come and go—
  The friends who have loved me so.
  They will come and go,
  And the ceaseless flow
  Of their laughter low,
And their merry talk will fill
The wonted haunts and places still.
  Will they perchance remember me,
  And sometimes name me lovingly?

Blind—Oh!—Blind.

Though clearest sunlight
  Shine about me day by day,
  Lighting all the onward way,
  Shaming cloud and storm away;
Ah! darkness and the dreariest night,
  Alone—I find—
  Blind—oh! blind.

Thoughts on Life.

We grope in darkness when we try
To solve this awful mystery.
Our souls round the enigma hover,
Yet Time nor trial doth discover
A single clue to trace the maze
That doth environ all our ways.

Days and weeks in swift succession
   Add their links unto Life's chain,
While the months, in long procession,
   Not so swiftly join the train;
Then the stately years approaching
   Glide in silence to their place,
Swell the numbers while encroaching
   Upon Life's allotted space.
Last the Cycles grandly numbered,
   Close the pageant sweeping by,
And the deeds which them have cumbered
   Roll to meet the Omniscient eye.

Cycles three God gives to mortals,
   Youth, Maturity and Age,
Each but leading to the portals,
   Whence we vanish from Time's stage.
Like a dream this world appeareth
   Some swift mockery of the brain
That in flashing disappeareth
   Never to return again,
When this human wrappage slowly
   Doth to earth resolve once more,
While the soul enfranchised—holy—
   To its promised Heaven doth soar.

The first Cycle—Human Childhood—
   When Life strays o'er flowery plains
With winged feet by stream or wildwood,
   Keeping time to summer rains;
Then each sense is thrilled with pleasure
   As the child doth onward bound,
In capricious speed or leisure
   Losing still no sight or sound.
In this Cycle gleams of Heaven
   Do the youthful heart entrance.

Glorious visions without leaven
    That no more shall meet its glance.

For Love—the Beautiful! now reigns
    With an absolute control,
Lures in lengths of gilded chains
    The unconscious, guileless soul.
Oh! it revels in a medium—
    Not the common air of earth—
Whose bright hues conceal the tedium
    That shall afterward have birth.
Golden Age! thou shinest divinely
    O'er the gloom of after years
Beaming through their aisles benignly
    Smiles that banish present tears.

Presaging heart! fain wouldst thou linger
    'Mid the blooms and joys of this,
But old Time's relentless finger
    Sternly glideth from such bliss.
Stay these moments thou mayst never,
    For more swiftly they flit by;
    Coming—going—go forever!

Now ye freighted years draw nigh!
    Lift your sable curtains flinging
Such a gloom upon the air—
    Ah! the heart knows ye are bringing
Struggles—grief—perhaps despair.

    .   .   .   .   .

Youth's glad hours have come and vanished;
    Morning rays are merged in noon;
Thoughts that we might once have banished
    Grow to fetters far too soon:
Tears that came like April showers,
    Cares that came like April glooms,
But to quicken Spring's fair flowers
    Into lovlier, sweeter blooms—
Ah! they drain bright eyes of gladness,
    Furrows delve on Youth's fair brow,
Transform joy into such sadness,
    Life nor charms nor cheats us now.

What doth meet us wheresoever
    We may turn appealing eyes?
Life's antagonisms forever
    Yield immutable replies.

THOUGHTS ON LIFE.

Sin and sorrow mingling darkly
   E'en beneath the fairest guise—
Fallen beings held up starkly,
   Illustrations for the wise—
Yet stainless little ones they were,
   Knelt at some dead mother's knee,
Lisped softly o'er the simple prayer,
   She told them reverently.

Want's pallid children crouching low
   Near by some Dives' door,
As Time's dissolving scenes this show
   Presenteth o'er and o'er,
Threadbare the garb of honest toil,
   A thatched roof for his head,
Life's struggles round his pathway coil
   And start beneath his tread;
While Indolence hath fine array;
   Muslins from India's looms—
Marvelous fabrics wrought they say
   In subterranean glooms.

There Persia's silks the eye beholds
   Of such rich and wondrous dyes,

Rainbows seem amid their folds
    Taking beautiful disguise.
Jewels rare are flashing brightly
    Where stained windows' mellow beams
Float through perfumed chambers lightly
    Flashing intercepted gleams!
These, Nature's adamantine tears,
    Shed o'er this fair fallen earth
Within some cavern's gloom through years,
    Slowly glistened into birth.

His roof some sculptor's hand hath wrought
    Into glorious tales of Art,
And it doth seem that Life hath brought
    All its blessings for his part;
Or elsewhere some earthly mixture
    Fashioned into manhood's form,
Fills some nook of life a fixture
    To some nobler being's harm—
Cunning in high places seated,
    Thrusteth honesty aside,
Laws by ermined vice are meted
    While afar virtue must bide.

Cycle this of swift transitions,
  And its tide bears heavy woes;
Life wears out by these attritions
  Time's long vistas near their close;
And Maturity descending,
  Finally Old Age sets in,
Silver hairs and wrinkles blending
  Till Death shall all cycles win.
Active into still life merges,
  Life s worn forces seek repose;
The Mind's labors, Passion's surges,
  And the Soul's sublime throes.

Torpor numbs or Age subdues them,
  Or Religion giveth balm,
Finding in this stage an emblem
  Of the future, holier calm.
Once our joy was lost in sorrow,
  Age now gently blends the twain;
Opposites a something borrow,
  Pleasure links itself with pain;
Love and Hope's anticipations
  Blighted by an early doom,

Some good angel's ministrations
   Nurse to kindly winter bloom.

And this is Life! And Death's dark stream
   Its Westward slope doth bound;
Nor may solution for the dream
   On this side Heaven be found.
What do we here, the weary heart
   In startled pauses oft doth ask;
Do we perform aright each part
   In our Life's apportioned task?
O, Life and Time and Change and Death,
   Swiftly your linked chain is run—
Ye come—ye go—a fleeting breath!
   Who your mystery hath won?

The Indians.

I saw them camped by the forest green,
Where its thickest branches made a screen
   From sun and wind for their wigwams rude;
With stolid mien and furtive air,
   A curious, sallow, dusky brood
The Red Men of the forest there.

They made their lodge by the far greenwood;
The women lazily gathered the wood,
   Heaped up the fires till their ruddy glow
Lit up faces that or young or old
   No trace of beauty or womanhood show,
No gleam of humanity's pure gold.

The Chiefs and Braves were scattered round,
Standing, sitting, stretched on the ground;
   Glances dark with the gloom of fate,
Milk-white teeth and coal-black hair,
   Forms of symmetry, tall and straight,
Faces wrinkled and seamed and spare.

I watched them, the somber, silent race,
Knowing no life but war and the chase;
   Watched for some revelation faint
Of their long descent and ancient line,
   Through gewgaws, feathers, scars and paint,
From the Jews of Palestine.

Plunged in ignorance, sloth and crime,
Curious link with creation's prime;
   The dawn of their far beginning lost
In a night of ages no stars illume;
   More surely than when strange waves they cross'd
They are onward borne to a direful doom.

A strange star glows in the eastern sky;
They mark it and shudder not knowing why;
   Swiftly it takes its westward way,
And lo! their wilderness blooms like the rose,
   As it scatters the night with its new born day,
And civilization's magic shows.

Cities throned on the hills are seen,
Villages dotting the plains between,

Countless vessels the rivers claim,
Steam cars remotest realms invade;
  For be it in glory, be it in shame,
The march of the white man can not be stayed.

So I watched them there by the far greenwood,
In a dreamy, half-prophetic mood ;
  As the forests that swiftly disappear,
As the snows that melt so soon in the sun,
  Their tribes are dwindling year by year,
And the Red Men's race is almost run.

Kansas.

["Oh, rare, rare earth!"—Mrs. Browning]

A WONDER-LAND, though one begot
In crimes and stripes that were forgot
But for their costly heritage;
Trailing its pitch on every page
That its historic pen doth trace
In hue no art may quite erase;
That makes her name a thing of scorn
Which good men mention but to warn,
Lest vice, grown arrogant, attain
Such tricks of gloss as hide its stain.
A wonder-land, how long, how long
Shall still your record flaunt such wrong?

A wonder-land, for all its harms
It matches with a thousand charms
Of prairie, sky, bluff, stream, and sun,
Ere the full year its course doth run.
Each season has its special place
And holds it with a special grace :—

Spring with her own, half shy, all sweet,
The tender grass springs swift to greet,
And where hath passed that dainty tread,
Lo! its green mantle overspread
With fleck of flower, bird, bee, whate'er
Is fair to see or sweet to hear.

A wonder-land, though summer shine
Not down on the ancestral pine,
Or roof-tree of a son she claims,
Or daughter, with their frontier fames,
But throngs of later children come
To seek her shelter and a home.
Did their far homes look on the sea?
The prairie shows like witchery.
Did music through those pine trees swell?
The long grass hath the self-same spell?
Of answering in melodies
Whatever mood of summer breeze.

A wonder-land, when Summer's reign
With Autumn's strives and strives in vain.
There comes, we know not how or why,

A change too subtle for the eye,
Of languid suns in golden haze,
And, lost in dreams, the long, still days.
Slow flashes through the drowsy air
As sleepy wings were droning there;
A crooning sound—a lullaby—
Where little brooks go creeping by.
O, Autumn-land, awake, asleep,
Men too but drowsy vigils keep.

A wonder-land, when Autumn wanes
And Winter its full sway attains;
Its snowy mantle spreading far
Without a break or fleck to mar
Its purity 'neath moon or sun.
This miracle when day is done:
To glowing pink the world we see
Even as we gaze change suddenly,
Carved in translucent, rosy light—
Then by degrees fade into night,—
Yet mark we not when sunset ends
And with the twilight softly blends.

The sunrise, too, a magic owns
Akin to that of Arctic zones.
The sun ablaze with splendor shows.
Sun-dogs, in circle, it enclose.
A sun-bow holds them in their place
To follow in the earth-round chase.
An atmosphere of myriad tints,
A shimmering mist of dazzling glints,
Of silvery points that swim, fall, rise,
Flash, glide, defy, and blind the eyes.
Spring, Summer, Autumn, Winter, each,
O, rare, rare Earth, your wonders teach.

O, wonder-land! O, land scarce known,
Where stretch vast prairies never mown
Save by wild herds and wilder fires
That change thy earth to funeral pyres,—
When on thee nature spreads her green,
And sunshine spreads its golden sheen—
From deepest depths of bluest skies
What marvel that enchanted eyes,
And bated breath, and pulse attest
The charms that thy new clime invest,

And that we turn from what has been
Some fairer future bent to win?

O, wonder-land, our Kansas, here
We cast thy horoscope, nor fear
From what thou hast already done
But that thy future shall outrun.
From all this moil and dawn of things
Hope's star, clear, steadfast, mighty springs—
Thy evil days shall pass away;
All we count greatest, best, shall sway;
High souls, clear heads, clean hands, sure feet,
In thy new generations meet;
And thou, begotten, born in sin,
A nobler era usher in.

Kansas, 1873.

Adrift.

I am out at sea
    All adrift—adrift—
And the sun goes down for only me
    On the clouds of the dawn uplift—
While strange strands flash and flicker away,
And strange isles gleam with the billows play,
And strange sails on the horizon glimmer,
And strange suns through the still air shimmer,
Till the whole world groweth strange to me
And I weary of being out at sea—
        Forever out at sea.

I am out at sea
    All adrift—adrift—
Yet I long till it ends in agony,
    To escape from this endless drift
To cool vales which my childhood bounded,
To green hillsides which upward rounded,

To the playmates sporting wildly there,
With shouts and laughter rending the air,
To the lapsing streams that whispered me
Not a word of warning of this sea
                Lying ahead for me.

      I am out at sea
         All adrift—adrift—
      Yet a dream comes often over me,
         And worlds not scenes seem to shift—
Of one in his manly prime and pride
Who claimed me with glance and voice his
    bride;
And then all the world was Paradise
Lit with the love in each other's eyes—
Not in stillest calm or sun's wax or wane
Caught I glimpse or sound of this dreary main,
            I sigh to escape in vain.

      I am out at sea
         All adrift—adrift—
      But that dream unfolds till I seem to see
         Children—just two—Heaven's own
            gift.

ADRIFT.

One I worshiped, he was like his sire,
A sculptor's model with soul of fire.
Claude claimed the other, he was most like me,
With golden brown hair and laugh of glee.
Ha! the blinding spray—I can not see—
It hath swept them away, leaving me
              Alone on this lonesome sea.

An Episode of Travel.

I sit alone and dream to-night
Of one, a brave young English knight,
A twelve month gone across the sea
I met—ah! does he think of me?

At night, at morn, at eve again,
We lingered with each other;—then—
His fate to go as mine to stay;—
The morrow—oh! how cold and gray.

For he was young and I was old;—
No sadder story can be told.
Forever, meant that dread good-bye.
To-night does he too dream and sigh?

A Madrigal.

Thou Star of my night, thou Star of my morn-
    ing,
Thou Light of my life, its pathway adorning,
    My wife, my Celeste.

Of men most forlorn all days lose their zest
When thou art afar—thou dearest and best,
    My wife, my Celeste.

Thou art coming, my own, lodestar of my life,
My sweetheart, my idol, mine only, my wife—
    My wife, my Celeste.

[Written for a friend whose wife had been absent some weeks and was coming home.]

Paolina,
The Little Orange Girl at Maiori, Gulf of Salerno.

She sings in the orange groves—
    Sings Paolina—
As hither and thither she roves
    Above the Marina;*
  Filling and swinging
  In time to her singing
Her basket till it can not hold
One more of those apples of gold.

She smiles in the orange groves—
    Smiles Paolina—
Which surely, prettily proves
    To "Signorina,"
  Catching shy glances
  As she advances
The little maid to be human,
Under the rustic all woman.

* Marina, quai.

PAOLINA.

She dreams in the orange groves—
    Dreams Paolina—
Blissful dreams coming in droves.
    That anellino *
    Which she caresses
    Mutely confesses
There is somewhere some one nearer
Yet than all others dearer.

She is gone—ah! the orange groves
    Miss Paolina—
Nevermore in them she roves
    Above the Marina.
    Is she still singing,
    Her sweet voice ringing
In chime with a baby band
Elsewhere in this sunny land?

* Anellino, ring.

Ludwig, der König! Louis, the King!
THE MAD KING OF BAVARIA.

Ludwig, der könig! Louis, the king!
These are the words that constantly ring
Soft and yet clear through my thoughts as I walk,
Soft and yet clear through my thoughts as I talk;—
  Ludwig, der könig! Louis, the king!

Ludwig, der könig! Louis, the king!
Just three little words, and yet how they ring
Over and over themselves in my brain,
Not quite a song, but a plaintive refrain;—
  Ludwig, der könig! Louis, the king!

Ludwig, der könig! Louis, the king!
I seem through the glamor the simple words fling

To see both a king—shall I say, and a man?
Who in the world's progress is found in the van;—
> Ludwig, der könig! Louis, the king!

Ludwig, der könig! Louis, the king!
How swift on the strain my fancy takes wing!
A king with the kingliest, kaiser or czar;
A man with the manliest, in peace or war;—
> Ludwig, der könig! Louis, the king!

Ludwig, der könig! Louis, the king!
Thy birthright of purple is no paltry thing;
And "noblesse oblige" has a might of its own
More mighty by far than a king on his throne;—
> Ludwig, der könig! Louis, the king!

Ludwig, der könig! Louis, the king!
To the son of thy sire his people must cling.
Oh! born to his greatness even more than his crown
Wilt not add to thyself a hero's renown?
> Ludwig, der könig! Louis, the king!

Ludwig, der könig! Louis, the king!
From the heart of thy people a great cry doth spring.
What is wanted? Not only a king at the helm
Of thy state, but a sire to both people and realm;—
  Ludwig, der könig! Louis, the king!

Ludwig, der könig! Louis, the king!
In some moment supreme weigh well this one thing!
Shrewd ruler, warm lover of science and art,
Thy subjects claim also a place in thy heart;—
  Ludwig, der könig! Louis, the king!

Ludwig, der könig! Louis, the king!
Beseech thee, think not these words mean a sting.
They only entreat thee the ancestral fame
Of the Wittelsbach House to increase by thy name;
  Ludwig, der könig! Louis, the king!

Munich, 1882.

Egypt.

This morning, glancing through a book,
   In pause of church-bell's chime,
The magic of a picture page
   Brought back a distant clime,
A clime of trance, and dream, and scene
   Of memories divine;
Of lotos' bloom, of desert's sheen,
   Ruin of sacred shrine,
In Egypt's burning, glowing gold
   Of tropical sunshine.

The stately palm tree's swaying plumes,
   The banyan's columned shade,
The shore washed by the river where
   The flocks of Ibis wade;
Or stand where land and water meet
   Nor sign of life betray,
While lapse the morns, the noons, the eves
   To twilights gold or gray—

Then with one impulse rise and cleave
    The air and fly away.

Mud villages sun-dried and brown
    With dove-cotes on the roof;
Chimneys like obelisks as tall,
    And many a quaint shadouf;
The weird shakiyeh's dismal drone
    That strikes the startled ear
With sighs and groans, and comes and goes,
    And echoes far and near;
While childlike, gentle *fellahs* watch
    And work, nor heed nor fear.

Along the banks phantoms of men
    And camels flit and fade—
A fez-capped Arab, turbaned Turk,
    Learned Copt, a blue-gowned maid,
A donkey and a donkey-boy,
    With gleaming teeth and smile,
Alert to catch one's leave to run
    Beside it mile on mile,
And scorning plaint of tire the way
    With prank and play beguile.

EGYPT.

The mountains rising near at hand,
   Those melting far away
In depths of distance, blue of sky,
   Or crystal of noon-day—
Alike the gazer wrap in bliss,
   And goad the searching thought
As they unroll their storied fronts
   In tomb and temple wrought,
When Egypt's great through ages thus
   Perennial memory sought.

Eons before the Parthenon
   The morning sunlight lit
Yon Doric column; and this one—
   The Lotos' counterfeit—
The rarest, fairest, just a flower
   In stone, uplifted there,
With all its loveliness revealed,
   Its grace beyond compare,
Has stood through cycles numberless
   In this enchanted air.

The Pyramids!—a catch of breath,
   A whirl of brain and sight,
A backward plunge toward Time's source
   In realms of endless night;—
The Sphynx!—the calm, impassive Sphynx!
   As in the dateless yore
Aloof from mortal sympathy,
   Defies as heretofore
All human questioning, and search,
   And will forevermore.

Oh! magic of a pictured page;
   Oh! wonder clime thus shown,—
Not home, not friends, not native land,
   Not strongest ties still known,
Can counteract thy witchery;
   A trance, a drift, a dream—
The soul escaped is floating down
   Old Nile's historic stream;
Entranced afar is taking in
   Bridge, palace, fane, hareem,

EGYPT.

Oh! hoary clime, Ancient of Days,
    Egypt, Time's oldest child,
How many rulers, each in turn,
    Thy glory have defiled.
The Fount of Learning centuries ere
    Its light elsewhere was shed,
To school, priest, temple, the wise men
    Of other lands were led.
That time recalling how submit
    To see thy glory fled?

The Alps.

It is those snow-crowned Monarchs I am thinking of,
  In their country far away,
As I bend both body and soul to hear
  What to each other they say.
There are strains sublime I can not interpret—
  Chants, hosannas, jubilees,
Carols, that rise and soar—and soar—and soar higher,
  In ecstatic harmonies.
In their Emyprean Solitude of air,
  Of sunlight, of mantling snow,
Of clashing clouds, forked lightning, hurtling thunder,
  Crashing avalanche, the flow—
The long, slow, noiseless, resistless, hidden, flow
  Of Glaciers' frozen streams,

Are they in sympathy with this life below?
  Or wrapped in supernal dreams?
Their voices that I catch, or—dream I do—
  Reach they to Stellar Spaces?
And mounting, widening, in the Music of the
    Spheres,
  Fill they appointed places?
They have such joyous, glad, ringing reso-
    nance,
  It pervades those realms remote;
So pure and cold—a burst of mingled har-
    mony
  Poured forth as from but one throat.
Chant they unconscious to Creation's ear,
  Peak answering unto peak?
Or the Great First Cause, Creator, Father, do
  They in praise and worship seek?
Watching the blue crystal bending o'er those
    heights,
  Spellbound, there wakes within a sense
Of kinship with beings *that are voices only*,
  Beings born of joys intense.

Gushes of song and hymns of Heaven's own
    choirs,
  Rise and float—a choral chain
Of melody unknown to mortal tongue and
    ear—
  Hope to capture which were vain.
Piercing entranced that dazzling distance but
    not
  With these human eyes of mine.
Something not myself yet myself escapes and
    joins
  Those far, formless forms divine.
Ye snow-capped Monarchs, how shall human
    speech express
  The miracles that crown you
Of viewless minstrels and of soundless min-
    strelsy,
  In that upper world of blue?
Even as I gaze, transfixed in awe and homage,
  Slowly slips the earth away,
And, some unknown force compelling, I seem
    upward borne
  To those realms of wondrous day;

While that other me, not me swiftly mingles
   With those shining hosts unseen,
Unheard, unfelt, but apprehended
   In that spirit-sphere serene.

Immortelles and Asphodels.
(Everlastings.)

THESE, our Earth's perennial flowers—
   The fadeless blooms by Poets sung,
Songs, that from Homer's Age till ours,
   Down the aisles of Time have rung—
In many an emblem do we weave
   For passionate Remembrance' sake;
And howe'er we joy, howe'er we grieve,
   Sacred pilgrimages make;
For Loss and Grief, the Asphodels
   On our graves we mourning lay;
For Memory, the Immortelles—
   Our loved ones live for us alway.
Death in Life, Life in Death—how we
This, Love's Faith, keep reverently.

www.ingramcontent.com/pod-product-compliance
Lightning Source LLC
Chambersburg PA
CBHW020150170426
43199CB00010B/972